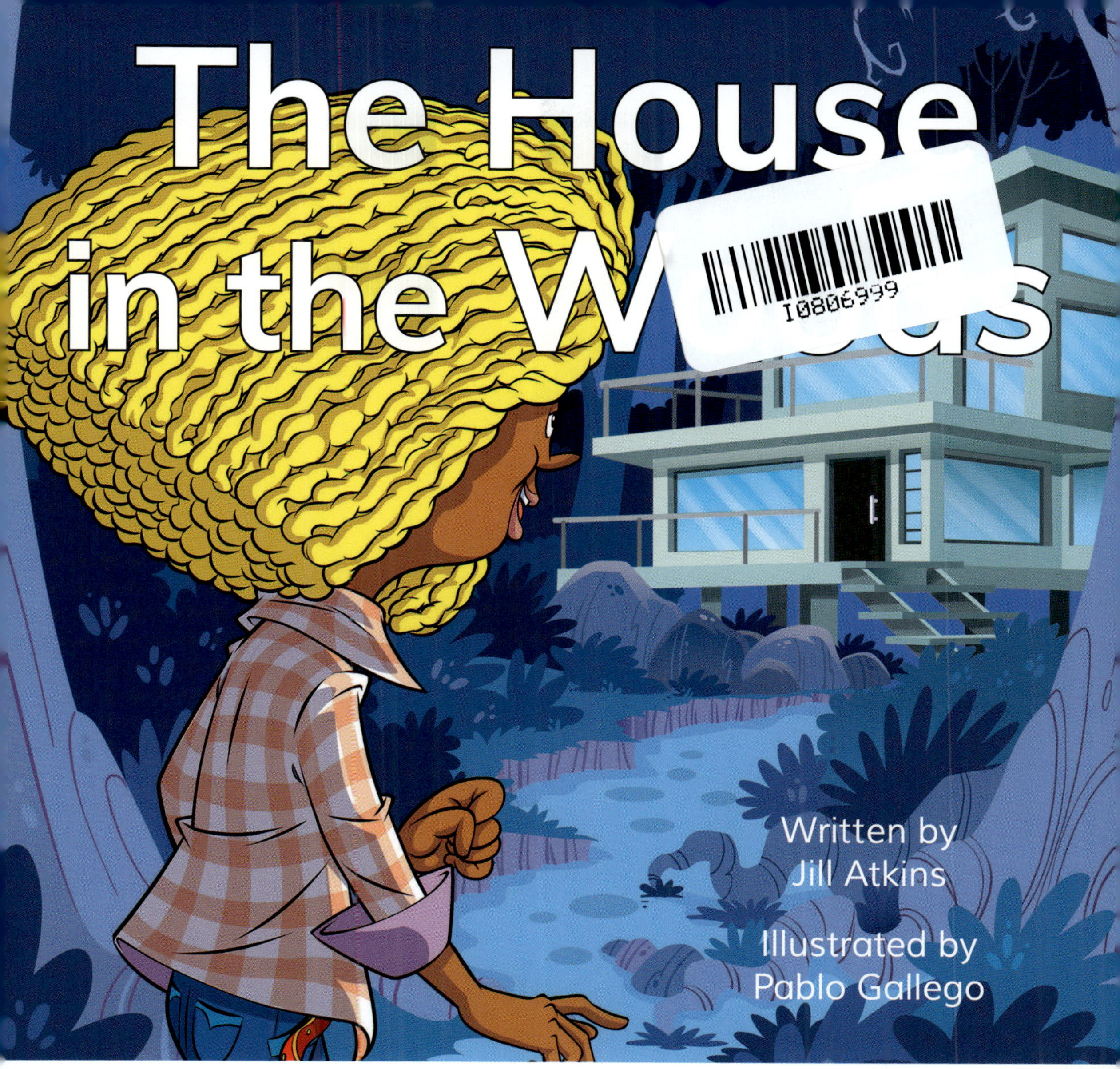

The House in the Woods

Written by
Jill Atkins

Illustrated by
Pablo Gallego

Published in 2026 by
Norwood House Press
2544 Clinton Street
Buffalo, NY 14224

Printed in the United States of America

Library of Congress Cataloging-in-Publication Data:
Names: Atkins, Jill (Children's author). | Gallego, Pablo, illustrator. | Harris, Carissa, illustrator.
Title: The house in the woods / written by Jill Atkins, illustrated by Pablo Gallego. Mega bucks / written by Jill Atkins, illustrated by Carissa Harris.
Description: Buffalo, NY : Norwood House Press, 2026. | Series: Phonics all-stars: phase 5c
Identifiers: ISBN 9781978578654 (pbk.) | ISBN 9781978578661 (library bound) | ISBN 9781978578678 (ebook)
Subjects: LCSH: Reading–Phonetic method–Juvenile literature. | English language–Phonetics–Juvenile literature. | Three bears (Tale)–Adaptation–Juvenile fiction. | Lottery winners–Juvenile fiction.
Classification: LCC LB1573.3 A796 2026 | DDC 372.465–dc23

CPSIA compliance information: Batch #CW26NHP: For further information contact Norwood House Press at 1-800-237-9932.

Goldylocks strolled into the dark forest.
She was looking for somewhere to rest.

Soon, she spied a little house.

"That looks perfect," she said.

She knocked, but no one was at home.

"Dare I go in?" she wondered.

She drew out her magic goose feather and waved it at the house. At once, she was inside

"How odd," she thought. "There are pictures of bears everywhere!"

Then she noticed three bowls of porridge.

The first bowl was much too hot. The second was too cold, but the third looked perfect.

"I'm hungry," thought Goldylocks, "and I don't care."

She waved her magic goose feather and suddenly **all** the bowls of porridge were just right.

Then she ate it all.

Then Goldylocks stared at the three chairs in the room.

"The first one is too big and square," she said. "But I'm too tired to look at the others."

She waved her goose feather and the first chair shrank to a perfect size.

As she sat down on it ... Crack! The chair broke.

"Oh, never mind!" laughed Goldylocks. "There was a lot of wear and tear on that chair. I am so tired, perhaps I need to find a bed."

There were three beds upstairs in the bears' bedroom.

The first bed was huge and the third was way too little. The second bed looked just right ... but Goldylocks had never tried a water bed.

So, with a whisk of the feather, the
second bed was suddenly a water bed.
Perfect!

Without a care, Goldylocks lay down on the bed.

In a moment, she was fast asleep.

She slept so soundly that she didn't hear the three bears come home.

She didn't hear Mr. Bear, Mrs. Bear, and Little Bear complaining about the empty porridge bowls.

She didn't hear Mr. Bear shouting that his chair was broken.

Most important, she didn't hear the three angry bears climbing the stairs and coming into the bedroom.

What will happen to Goldylocks?
Is this the end of her story?

No!

Suddenly, Goldylocks jumped up.

"You don't scare me!" she cried, as she waved her magic goose feather at the bears.

Sizzly fizz! The bears vanished in a puff of smoke.

Goldylocks smiled and wrapped one of the bears' dressing gowns around her. Then she went downstairs.

How good it was to have a new home of her own!

She mended Mr. Bear's chair and sat down, pleased with her day.

Soon it would be lunchtime ...

Mega Bucks

Written by
Jill Atkins

Illustrated by
Carissa Harris

It was the night of the draw.

No one had won it for a month, so this week the jackpot was massive.

“Here we go,” squealed my sister, Tamsin, as the balls began to drop.

“Yes!” Mom exclaimed, as the first ball matched her numbers.

The second and third balls matched too.

"Stay calm," said Dad. "We are halfway there."

When the final ball dropped, we went berserk!

We had six matching balls! We had won mega bucks!

Soon it was spend, spend, spend!

Mom had a talk with Dad.

"I want the most expensive house on the market," she told him. "With cream walls."

We ended up with a monster of a house.
Just the hall was as big as our old place.

Next, Mom got a flashy sports car.

Dad chose a big pickup truck. He'd wanted a pickup for years.

Then he purchased the local soccer club. There was new gear for the team.

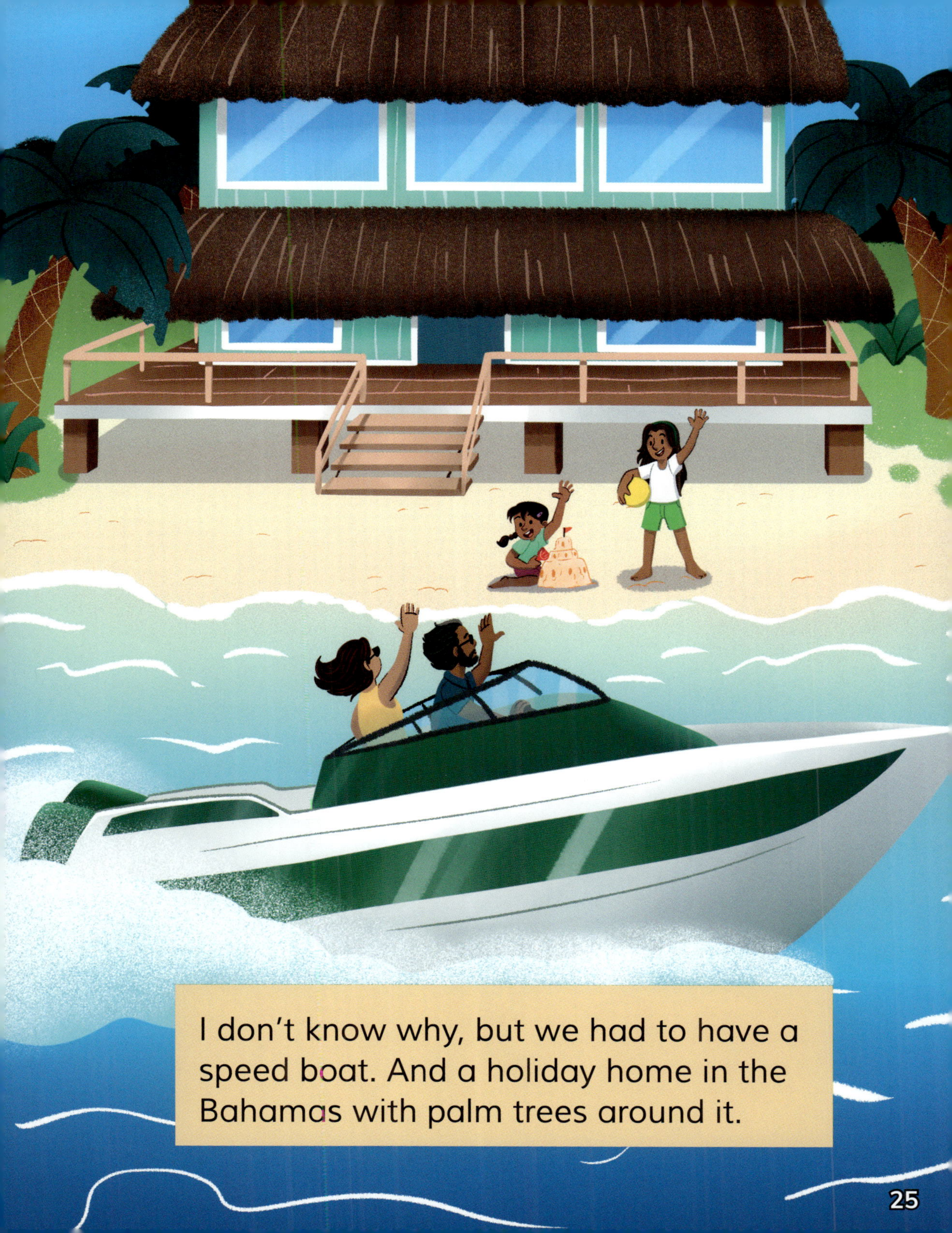

I don't know why, but we had to have a speed boat. And a holiday home in the Bahamas with palm trees around it.

Then, to my horror, Tamsin and I were sent off to a swanky school.

Overnight, we lost all the friends we'd had for years.

But that was only half of it. The kids at the new school called us rude names.

Then the fights started.

Mom blamed Dad. Dad yelled at us. We yelled back.

I wanted my old life back.

One day, I found Mom crying in the hall.

"I've half a mind to return to that little house," she wailed.

"Then why don't we?" I asked.

We sold the monster house and the home in the Bahamas.

Dad swapped his truck for a normal car.

Mom and Dad donated loads to charity too.

We purchased a little house on the same street as the old one.

Was I pleased to be walking back into my old school?

Not at first, but now, a few months later, things are just like they used to be.

Am I happy? Oh yes. I have my friends back.

Do we still bother with the lottery?
What do you think?